The Quotation Bank f[illegible]

The Great Gatsby

F Scott Fitzgerald

First published in 2022 by:
The Quotation Bank
Esse Publishing Limited
10 9 8 7 6 5 4 3 2

A CIP catalogue record for this book is available from the British Library.
ISBN 978-1-9999816-7-9

All enquiries to: contact@thequotationbank.co.uk

Printed and bound by Target Print Limited, Broad Lane, Cottenham, Cambridge CB24 8SW.

www.thequotationbank.co.uk

Introduction

Quotations

Revision and Essay Planning

Welcome to The Quotation Bank, the comprehensive guide to all the key quotations you need to succeed in your exams.

Whilst you may have read the novel, watched a film adaptation, understood the plot and have a strong grasp of context, all questions in your A-Levels require you to write a focused essay, full of textual references and quotations (be they textual, critical or contextual), and most importantly, quotations that you then analyse.

I think we all agree it is analysis that is the tricky part – and that is why we are here to help!

The Quotation Bank takes 25 of the most important quotations from the text, interprets them, analyses them, highlights literary techniques Fitzgerald has used, puts them in context, and suggests which quotations you might use in which essays. We have also included 10 contextual and critical quotations, analysed them, and linked them closely to the text, all for you to explore.

At the end of **The Quotation Bank** we have put together a critical history and great revision exercises to help you prepare for your exam. We have also included a detailed glossary to make sure you completely understand what certain literary terms actually mean!

How The Quotation Bank can help you in your exams.

The Quotation Bank is designed to make sure every point you make in an essay clearly fulfils the Assessment Objectives an examiner will be using when marking your work.

Every quotation comes with the following detailed material:

Interpretation: The interpretation of each quotation allows you to fulfil **AO1**, articulating an informed, personal response, and **AO5**, using different interpretations to inform your exploration of the text.

Techniques: Using associated concepts and terminology (in this case, the techniques used by Fitzgerald) is a key part of **AO1**, and can help you identify and analyse ways in which meanings are shaped (**AO2**).

Analysis: We have provided as much analysis (**AO2**) as possible, as well as exploring the significance and influence of contextual material (**AO3**) and different interpretations (**AO5**). It is a great idea to analyse the quotation in detail – you need to do more than just say what it means, but also try to explore a variety of different ways of interpreting it.

Use in essays on…Your answer needs to be focused to fulfil **AO1**. This section helps you choose relevant quotations and link them together for a stronger, more detailed essay.

How to use The Quotation Bank.

Many students spend time learning quotations by heart. This can be useful, but it is important to remember what you are meant to do with quotations once you get into the exam.

By using **The Quotation Bank**, not only will you have a huge number of textual, critical and contextual quotations to use in your essays, you will also have ideas on what to say about them, how to analyse them, how to link them together, and what questions to use them for.

These quotations can form the basis of your answer, making sure every point articulates an informed, personal response **(AO1)** and allows you to analyse ways in which meanings are shaped **(AO2)**.

The critical and contextual quotations allow you to easily and effectively explore the significance and influence of context **(AO3)**, and provide you with a variety of different readings to explore **(AO5).**

The textual quotations cover the whole text to allow you to show comprehensive whole text knowledge, and the critical and contextual quotations cover the full range of the text's publication history to help you explore the contexts in which the text was both written and received **(AO3)**.

Chapter One:

"I'm inclined to reserve all judgements."

Interpretation: Nick is the character invented to write the novel we read; it is important to remember everything that happens in the story is filtered through his character's perspective. Nick attempts to paint himself as an objective and non-judgmental person.

Techniques: Narrative Voice; Language.

Analysis:

- Nick contradicts his claims to be non-judgemental, admitting he "feigned sleep" when people confided in him in the past. He later views Gatsby's life with "unaffected scorn" and admits he is "disgusted" by Tom and Daisy's marriage.
- Furthermore, he judges Myrtle for her haughty behaviour in New York at the apartment; whilst he is keen to tell us he does not immediately judge others, he spends the rest of the novel explicitly doing so.
- Ironically, the only person Nick exempts from judgement appears to be Gatsby. These comments make the reader less trusting of his narration; they suggest he is dishonest, contradictory, insecure, and lacks self-awareness.

Use in essays on… Morality; Identity; Class; Wealth.

Chapter One:

"What foul dust floated in the wake of his [Gatsby's] dreams."

Interpretation: Gatsby's dream was tarnished and unachievable before he even began, constantly pursued by a lingering "foul dust".

Techniques: Foreshadowing; Imagery.

Analysis:

- "Dust" taints and smothers Gatsby's dream. The imagery of "foul dust" symbolises the American Dream itself as an illusion that men blindly build their lives upon, only to discover it is as intangible as "dust", simply a myth.
- Nick highlights that Gatsby's dream was tainted before it began, with "dust" and "wake" both having religious connotations of death; later in the novel Myrtle is literally returned to the "dust" in pursuit of her dreams, whilst no one attends Gatsby's "wake" after his dream ends.
- The reader may question Gatsby's sense of naivety in following something, whether it be Daisy or the American Dream, which was futile ("dreams").

Use in essays on... American Dream; Desire; Obsession.

Chapter One:

"It was a factual imitation of some Hotel de Ville in Normandy, with a tower on one side."

Interpretation: Nick's description highlights how Gatsby's house, much like his entire character, is not real. It's a copy of a "Hotel de Ville in Normandy", with the faux-European history trying to create a sense of tradition and validation to Gatsby's heritage.

Techniques: Imagery; Setting; Juxtaposition.

Analysis:

- The imagery created by "Hotel de Ville" and "tower on one side" links to the idea of a fairytale castle, unreal and fantastical.
- The juxtaposition of "factual" and "imitation" is almost oxymoronic – authenticity is always tainted by an underlying sense of falsity.
- Gatsby fashions himself as Daisy's 'Prince Charming' during the novel, until Tom's realisation in Chapter Seven that Gatsby is trying to take Daisy away from him; he challenges Gatsby and it becomes clear she will not leave Tom.

Use in essays on…Obsession; Illusion; Identity; American Dream.

Chapter One:

"Drifted here and there unrestfully wherever people played polo and were rich together."

Interpretation: Despite their family connections, Nick makes a damning judgement on Tom and Daisy Buchanan's lack of direction and purpose.

Techniques: Tone; Adverb; Alliteration.

Analysis:

- Nick's statement implies the rich are an elite group, secluded by their wealth from the rest of society, operating on a different level to the rest of the populace. The use of "drifted" and "unrestfully" evokes the boredom and lack of direction Fitzgerald criticised in the life of the landed rich in post-war society.
- Nick appears to condemn this behaviour, setting himself apart from those he shares a similar background with; the alliteration of the 'p' in "people played polo" creates a dismissive, belittling tone.
- Tom's restlessness arguably causes him to seek affairs which further distances him from Daisy; she is aware of these affairs and it builds resentment. The post-war generation were seen as disorientated and directionless ("drifted"), living a hedonistic lifestyle which lacked moral purpose.

Use in essays on… Wealth; Class; Society; Materialism.

Chapter One:

"He stretched out his arms toward the dark water in a curious way, and, far as I was from him, I could have sworn he was trembling. Involuntarily I glanced seaward – and distinguished nothing except a single green light, minute and far away…"

Interpretation: Fitzgerald sets up Gatsby's characterisation, linking him explicitly to Daisy. He purchased a house across the bay only to attract her with his grandiose parties.

Techniques: Imagery; Symbolism; Foreshadowing.

Analysis:

- The imagery of Gatsby stretching his arms towards the light emphasises his physical distance from Daisy, with "dark water" foreshadowing troubled times.
- "Trembling" evokes a sense of desperation to reach Daisy (he is "trembling" later when they meet at Nick's house). The light being electric and artificial highlights the love he has for Daisy (and indeed Daisy herself) is also artificial.
- Coming at the end of the chapter, Fitzgerald delays Gatsby's introduction and his obsession with Daisy. In creating a damning portrait of her character in this chapter, Fitzgerald questions Gatsby's love for such a person.

Use in essays on…Love; Obsession; American Dream; Wealth.

Chapter Two:

"She smiled slowly and, walking through her husband as if he were a ghost, shook hands with Tom, looking him flush in the eye."

Interpretation: On meeting Myrtle, Nick's descriptions are less than complimentary. He implies a connection between Tom and Myrtle that has already been established.

Techniques: Language; Simile; Juxtaposition.

Analysis:

- Myrtle's negative treatment of her husband ("walking through her husband"), and Nick describing him to be like "a ghost", suggests he has no substance to him, as if he is not present, simply hanging around in an unwanted fashion.
- On the other hand, her assertive interaction with Tom, "looking him flush in the eye" and "shook hands", is daring and certainly belies the fact this is not the first time they have met.
- Myrtle's atypical assertive behaviour evokes her determination to improve her life and leave the Valley of Ashes, using her own "vitality" and the affair with Tom to do so; the sibilance of "she smiled slowly" is strong and determined.

Use in essays on... Class; Desire; American Dream; Power.

Chapter Three:

"Yellow cocktail music."

Interpretation: There are many references to light and colour at Gatsby's numerous parties, especially references which seem to convey a sense of artificiality.

Techniques: Synesthesia; Tone.

Analysis:

- Combined with "cocktail", "yellow" implies the music is frivolous and creates an atmosphere of frippery. This could suggest to a reader that the party, and the guests themselves, are just for show, garish and shallow.
- Throughout the passage the reader gets a sense that Nick tends to look down on these people as they are overly concerned with appearances and wealth.
- Fitzgerald's depictions of Gatsby's parties and those who attend are designed to critique the post-war, materialistic society, suggesting that they are "like moths", drawn to and blinded by Gatsby's "coloured lights", and as such have no moral fibre nor live in the real world.

Use in essays on…Materialism; Class; Society; Illusion.

Chapter Three:

"Sometimes they came and went without having met Gatsby at all."

Interpretation: Fitzgerald creates an air of mystery around Gatsby, delaying his arrival until Chapter Three. He implies no one ever "met" the authentic Gatsby, in part because there isn't one; he is a reinvention of Jay Gatz, a character drawn to some degree from the figure of Dan Cody.

Techniques: Language; Verb Usage.

Analysis:

- Gatsby is portrayed in different lights. He is described almost as royalty ("signed Jay Gatsby in a majestic hand"), "an Oxford man", "in the American army" where he "killed a man", and even "a spy" related to Kaiser Wilhelm.
- It's ironic then, that at the same time as being surrounded by so many people at his parties, Fitzgerald clearly creates an air of isolation around Gatsby who is, "standing alone on the marble steps and looking from one group to another".
- Indeed, when Nick first meets him, Gatsby recognises him first ("Your face is familiar") but Nick doesn't recognize Gatsby at all before he is taken off to answer a phone call.

Use in essays on... Identity; American Dream; Materialism, Isolation.

Chapter Three:

"It's a bona-fide piece of printed matter. It fooled me. This fella's a regular Belasco. It's a triumph. What thoroughness!"

Interpretation: Nick emphasizes Owl Eyes' shocked reaction to Gatsby's library being filled with real books and "bona-fide piece[s] of printed matter". He alludes to David Belasco, a famous theatre producer, well known for his intensely realistic stages and sets.

Techniques: Language; Allusion; Foreshadowing.

Analysis:

- Nick notes the library is "panelled with carved English Oak" to make Gatsby's house appear like older mansions of established aristocratic families, a hint there is something unreal about the "thoroughness" of both Gatsby's house and life.
- Owl Eyes notes the illusory nature ("fooled me") of Gatsby and his house; he mutters if "one brick was removed the whole library was liable to collapse", which suggests he feels it is a façade, a metaphor for the whole of Gatsby's life.
- Fitzgerald makes the wider point that if one "brick" of Gatsby's outward image were to falter, the entire illusion would shatter, foreshadowing how Gatsby's life will fall apart later in the novel.

Use in essays on…Illusion; American Dream; Identity; Materialism.

Chapter Four:

"On Sunday, while church bells rang…the world and its mistress returned to Gatsby's house."

Interpretation: Fitzgerald highlights Christian religion and morality ("church") has been replaced with the new religion that is hedonism and capitalism ("Gatsby's house").

Techniques: Hyperbole; Idiom.

Analysis:

- The "church bells rang" as people go, not to church, but to Gatsby's party. "Sunday" is a traditional day of rest and spirituality – the fact people went "while church bells rang" highlights their explicit rejection of the church.
- Fitzgerald further highlights the hedonistic and patriarchal nature of society through the idiom "world and its mistress", hyperbolically underlining the lack of morality and monogamy in society at the time.
- The secularisation of society could be as a result of World War I, where people had seen such horrors that they felt a lack of faith in religion itself.

Use in essays on…Class; Materialism; American Dream; Wealth.

Chapter Four:

"Finest specimens of human molars."

Interpretation: Wolfsheim's relationship with Gatsby confirms his wealth has been achieved through nefarious means, horrifically evidenced as Wolfsheim wears parts of his previous associates as "specimens" or warnings to others of his reputation.

Techniques: Language.

Analysis:

- Wolfsheim is based on Arnold Rothstein, who fixed the 1919 World Series, one of Wolfsheim's accomplishments that "staggered" Nick. Nick reacts with prejudice towards the Jewish character, betrayed in descriptions of his "tiny eyes in the half darkness", a bias against the foreign "Other" prevalent in the so-called respectable society of the time (see Tom's earlier "Goddard" comments).
- Wolfsheim's criminality is visibly on show with "human molars", in contrast with Gatsby's secrecy, stressing both the luxury and corruption of the Jazz Age.
- Tom Buchanan also being present conveys that even outwardly respectable people ignored Prohibition laws. Whilst Tom may not have "specimens" on show, Fitzgerald portrays New York's corruption spreading throughout society.

Use in essays on…Power; Morality.

Chapter Five:

"When I came home to West Egg that night I was afraid for a moment that my house was on fire."

Interpretation: Nick comments on Gatsby's house, so lit up with an ostentatious display of wealth, that it conjures destructive connotations of "fire" rather than a lively party.

Techniques: Metaphor; Setting.

Analysis:

- East Egg symbolises old money and long-established generations of wealth – the 'royalty' of New York. Apparently conservative and aristocratic, they are not as refined as it appears; indeed, they are fashionable but fake.
- Its appealing surface hides unattractive realities; the Buchanan's marriage is an unhappy one, and Daisy's looks and wealth make for a bored, cynical and empty interior. West Egg is where the nouveau riche live, typified by excessive displays of wealth that lack taste, such as Gatsby's yellow car and beacon-like house.
- The house alight ("on fire") is metaphorical, a beacon designed to attract the moth-like Daisy over the bay to his party and into his arms. Instead, it creates an uncomfortable fear in Nick ("afraid for a moment").

Use in essays on…Wealth; Obsession; Desire; Illusion.

Chapter Five:

"Luckily the clock took this moment to tilt dangerously at the pressure of his head, whereupon he turned and caught it with trembling fingers, and set it back in place."

Interpretation: Gatsby is uneasy about meeting Daisy in what is a deeply awkward moment where Gatsby loses his calm veneer – even time seems against him.

Techniques: Symbolism.

Analysis:

- Knocking the clock off and catching it mid-air symbolises Gatsby's wish to pause time so he can be with Daisy, or to make up for lost time in this moment at Nick's house, yet it is so close to slipping through his "trembling fingers."
- Gatsby's self-belief in "can't repeat the past? Why of course you can!" becomes a hamartia; he has a delusional, naive sense of reality which causes "trembling", "pressure" and things to "tilt dangerously", foreshadowing his downfall.
- Fitzgerald warns about dreams not living up to reality; Nick notes Daisy "tumbled short of his dreams". Readers are asked to question here if ever the reality can live up to the dream – are things not best left "back in place"?

Use in essays on…American Dream; Desire; Obsession; Illusion; Love.

Chapter Six:

"The rock of the world was founded securely on a fairy's wing."

Interpretation: The imagery in this statement serves to highlight the fragility of Gatsby's dream, secured on a foundation of nothing more than a "fairy's wing".

Techniques: Metaphor; Juxtaposition.

Analysis:

- A "fairy's wing" is magical yet breakable. The metaphor highlights his dream is settled on something fragile or unrealistic. Fitzgerald here perhaps proposes that the American Dream creates the fantastical potential to fly yet, in reality, it is fragile - the stuff of fairy tales. It is not available in the real world.
- Daisy's maiden name, "Fay", is Old English for fairy and thus highlights Gatsby bases his life choices on things which do not really exist in the real world.
- The juxtaposition of "rock", "founded" and "securely" with the foundations sitting "on a fairy's wing" emphasise the precarious nature of the "world" Gatsby has created for himself.

Use in essays on…Illusion; Obsession; American Dream; Desire.

Chapter Six:

"'She used to be able to understand...' He broke off and began to walk up and down a desolate path of fruit rinds and discarded favors and crushed flowers."

Interpretation: Nick illustrates Gatsby's extreme capacity to delude himself; neither Gatsby nor society can go back.

Techniques: Imagery; Symbolism.

Analysis:

- The imagery of the "desolate path" is symbolic of the notion Gatsby has lost his way; the path to his dream is tarnished and hidden now.
- As the path is covered in "discarded favors" and "fruit rinds", it implies that, like the parties, his love is gone. The "crushed flowers" are key as Daisy has been described as a flower previously; however, here the description is negative, symbolic of his "crushed" hopes and dreams.
- "Walk up and down" illustrates his boundless capacity for hope; Gatsby keeps moving, still refusing to acknowledge his hope of a reconciliation with Daisy, and by association achieving his American Dream, is actually "crushed".

Use in essays on...American Dream; Desire; Illusion; Materialism.

Chapter Seven:

"She realized at last what she was doing—and as though she had never, all along, intended doing anything at all."

Interpretation: Caught in the reality of being found to be having an affair, Daisy "realized" she cannot be with Gatsby, or gamble his new wealth and questionable business practices for the security of her protective 'old money' wealth and status.

Techniques: Language; Repetition.

Analysis:

- "Realized" highlights Daisy has deluded herself over her affair with Gatsby, perhaps as revenge for Tom's affairs, yet finally understands, in reality, she cannot leave him and have the same financial security.
- It could be argued Daisy gives up on her own personal desires and opts for material desire with Tom. On the other hand, "never…intended" implies that Daisy is indeed highly materialistic; she "never" had an intention of leaving.
- She previously "cried stormily" over Gatsby's shirts which reflects the shallow capitalist ideology of the wealthy, but the repetition of "doing" highlights the futility of Daisy's life; all she is ever capable of are passive actions such as crying over clothes, and she has no real autonomy.

Use in essays on…Gender; Illusion.

Chapter Seven:

"Picking up Wilson like a doll."

Interpretation: The lower classes are frequently abused by the wealthy throughout the novel; Tom has an affair with Myrtle to resolve his ennui and restlessness, but the brutal consequences are now evident. Myrtle has "her life violently extinguished" and is left with her breast "swinging loose like a flap"; Wilson becomes "like a doll".

Techniques: Simile.

Analysis:

- Tom has used the Wilsons; Myrtle for sex, George as a cheap mechanic who becomes desperate for his business. Both share the same misplaced belief that Tom will help provide the social mobility they so ardently desire.
- Wilson's devastation at his wife's death renders him almost as lifeless as Myrtle, dehumanized and "like a doll". In death, much like in life, Tom treats the Wilsons as toys, playthings for him to play with, manipulate and control.
- Even at Wilson's darkest moment, when in need of "picking up", Tom uses it reprehensibly to his advantage to control and misguide Wilson's actions, ultimately seeking his revenge on Gatsby.

Use in essays on…Morality; Power.

Chapter Eight:

"I waited, and about four o'clock she came to the window and stood there for a minute and then turned out the light."

Interpretation: Daisy "turned out the light" during Gatsby's hero-quest/stalker vigil outside her home. Her actions demonstrate her active choice to remain with Tom.

Techniques: Symbolism; Juxtaposition.

Analysis:

- Fitzgerald uses light being "turned out" as a symbol in juxtaposition to the "green light" of hope in Chapter One.
- Daisy symbolically "turned out the light" on their relationship and, by association, Gatsby's dreams. He refuses to recognize the reality of the situation and "waited". Whilst it reminds us of the capacity for hope in a fractured, aimless society, ultimately this dream is an illusion, flawed and unachievable, and leads to his tragic downfall in his refusal to see clearly through the "window".
- Interestingly, "four o'clock" recurs at significant points in the novel: Daisy is reunited with Gatsby at four o'clock in Chapter Five; he later dies at around four in the afternoon.

Use in essays on... Obsession; Desire; Power; Isolation.

Chapter Eight:

"Committed himself to the following of a grail."

Interpretation: Nick romanticises Gatsby's feelings for Daisy by elevating Gatsby's obsession to that of a heroic quest, a chivalrous pursuit.

Techniques: Imagery; Allusion.

Analysis:

- Religious imagery of "grail" portrays Daisy as a sacred object to be discovered, sought after and possessed.
- Daisy is Gatsby's holy "grail", turned into a religious icon, which he imbues with magical and spiritual properties. In Chapter Five, Daisy cannot remember how long it has been since they have seen each other; Gatsby quickly blurts out "five years". This creates an inevitable tone of awkwardness, as the meeting clearly holds far more weight for Gatsby than Daisy.
- His loyalty in following her is similar to the knight's quest that "grail" alludes to; instead of armour, Gatsby wears his colourful shirts, and his horse is his pretentious car.

Use in essays on…Desire; Obsession; Materialism; American Dream.

Chapter Eight:

"Gatsby was overwhelmingly aware of the youth and mystery that wealth imprisons and preserves, of the freshness of many clothes and of Daisy, gleaming like silver, safe and proud above the hot struggles of the poor."

Interpretation: This description conveys not only the unfairness of the class system in America, but also the supposed limitations that even enormous wealth can bring.

Techniques: Imagery; Irony; Simile.

Analysis:

- The noun "imprisons" is ironic; it is the wealthy here who are allegedly not free, suggesting wealth is a trap. The aimless rich are caught in their world of appearances and "the freshness of many clothes".
- Daisy is objectified, presented as attractive by Gatsby through the simile "gleaming like silver" as a trophy, and as something separated from the "poor".
- The "hot struggles of the poor" are portrayed as an almost noble pursuit, something empowering, perhaps because it mirrors the early exhausting work of the original pioneers. However, the dream of wealth is an illusion, unavailable to the underclass even though they work hard to achieve it. Although "wealth imprisons", it also keeps people "safe and proud above".

Use in essays on…Wealth; Class; Materialism.

Chapter Eight:

"Gatsby shouldered the mattress."

Interpretation: To truly fulfil the role of tragic hero, Gatsby needs to have an epiphany; a moment of total clarity in which he finds enlightenment and accepts his flaw. Nick tries to bestow one upon him in his narration, but it is unclear if Gatsby ever sees the truth.

Techniques: Imagery; Allusion.

Analysis:

- The description of "shouldered the mattress" could be an allusion to Christ carrying his crucifix, presenting Gatsby very much as an innocent victim.
- It is autumn, signifying death. Continuing the spiritual imagery, in his time in the pool, Gatsby is symbolically cleansed of the sins of materialism, and Nick imagines him having a moment of true realisation.
- This is a counterpoint to his earlier rechristening on the lake as his false persona of Jay Gatsby. He waits for Daisy's call until 4 o'clock, the time of his death; he clings until the very last to the idea that Daisy will somehow choose him.
- Gatsby's obsession with Daisy is here presented as a burden to be "shouldered", something he carried up to the point of death.

Use in essays on…Identity; Illusion; American Dream; Isolation.

Chapter Eight:

"He must have felt that he had lost the old warm world… he must have looked up at an unfamiliar sky through frightening leaves and shivered as he found what a grotesque thing a rose is and how raw the sunlight was upon the scarcely cut grass."

Interpretation: Nick imagines how Gatsby's epiphany made him see the stark reality of the world; the truth has burst through the "unfamiliar sky".

Techniques: Imagery; Motif.

Analysis:

- Fitzgerald uses the motif of flowers (the "grotesque…rose" and "frightening leaves") and nature to present Gatsby's newly unsentimental view of the world.
- Nick suggests roses aren't inherently beautiful; people in the "old warm world" choose to view them that way. Daisy is "grotesque" in the same way; Gatsby has invested her with beauty and meaning by making her the "silver" object of his dream. It is Gatsby then who has increased Daisy's value and importance; without him she would merely be yet another idle, rich young woman.
- His epiphany is highlighted in the "raw[ness]" of the "sunlight", reflecting the harsh view of reality he now has, almost too painful to look at. Nick believes Gatsby finally realised the uncompromising gritty truth before his death.

Use in essays on…American Dream; Illusion; Desire; Obsession.

Chapter Nine:

"They were careless people, Tom and Daisy – they smashed up things and creatures and then retreated back into their money or their vast carelessness, or whatever it was that kept them together and let other people clean up the mess they had made."

Interpretation: Nick is no longer "inclined to reserve all judgements"; he certainly judges people at the end of the novel, condemning Tom and Daisy for the way they "smashed up things" and then "retreated back into their money".

Techniques: Repetition; Listing.

Analysis:

- Nick stresses that wealth protects the rich, and the capitalist society as a whole demonstrates no social responsibility. Wealth is a protective advantage used to "clean up" their sins. "Carelessness" is repeated here, presented as a state of being for the rich where wealth allows them to commit immoral acts ("smashed up") without retribution – responsibility falls to "other people".
- The list structure adds emphasis to Nick's tone of disgust, serving as an accumulation of negative points about the Buchanans. Here Fitzgerald presents a chilling indictment of post-war society as immoral and inhumane.

Use in essays on…Morality; Inequality; American Dream; Wealth.

Chapter Nine:

"I went over and looked at that huge incoherent failure of a house…the inessential houses began to melt away…the old island here that flowered once for Dutch sailors' eyes - a fresh green breast of the new world."

Interpretation: Nick's view of East and West evolves throughout the novel. After Gatsby's death the East coast becomes "haunted" and "distorted" for him since he saw the moral decay and the hollowness, futility and loss of the American Dream.

Techniques: Symbolism; Imagery.

Analysis:

- Gatsby failed ("huge incoherent failure") in gaining the dream; it was hollow ("inessential") all along. Gatsby hosted a series of "gleaming, dazzling parties" that suggest a glittering surface but little underneath. The East is revealed as a place lacking morals, focused on amassing wealth and using others to keep it.
- Nick imagines it was once "a fresh green breast", suggesting innocence and hope, holding promise for the initial explorers, a paradise of endless potential, with a "breast" to give succour to the new world. Ironically, Myrtle is described viscerally as having her breast torn in the crash, perhaps highlighting the suffering America itself will face from those who live off it.

Use in essays on…American Dream; Illusion; Desire; Identity.

Chapter Nine:

"Gatsby believed in the green light, the orgastic future that year by year recedes before us…So we beat on, boats against the current, borne back ceaselessly into the past."

Interpretation: Gatsby's dream was over before it started; however, it is human nature to "beat on" and keep reaching for that imagined future.

Techniques: Language; Symbolism.

Analysis:

- Nick's narrative of Gatsby's story ends by referring back to Chapter One's "green light", creating a "ceaselessly" cyclical structure to the narrative.
- The cyclical nature of hopes and dreams implies the endless nature of humans striving for a future they can never achieve. Gatsby believed in the dream symbolised by the "green light", but Fitzgerald indicates that, paradoxically, the more people work towards it, the further it "recedes before us".
- Gatsby represents humanity's ("we" and "us") endless capacity for hope. The image of the boats in the "ceaseless tide" captures the juxtaposition of futility and hope – a cycle repeating itself.

Use in essays on…Desire; American Dream; Power; Obsession.

Thomas Parke D'Invilliers (1920), the fictitious protagonist of Fitzgerald's *This Side of Paradise*, advises,

"Then wear the gold hat."

Interpretation: The epigraph at the beginning of the novel comes from Fitzgerald's *This Side of Paradise*. The speaker, Thomas Parke D'Invilliers, is a poet who ignores the grittier side of life, as Gatsby does, hiding behind a veneer of wealth and "gold".

Analysis:

- The epigraph gives advice on how to win over a girl, utilising a hyperbolic image reflecting Gatsby and Daisy's story. It advises, as Gatsby does obsessively, going out of his way to impress Daisy with his wealth and status.
- This is symbolised by the "gold hat", and through his bold deeds, described metaphorically as aiming to "bounce high". It advises that whatever Gatsby can possibly do to attract her attention is worthwhile if it wins Daisy.
- The fact it is a hat to "wear" represents Gatsby, who uses his wealth to put on a façade; this spectacle, however, is just that. Similar to all the distractions he surrounds himself with, be it parties, mirrors on his car, colourful shirts and attempts to convince people he was an "Oxford man"", Fitzgerald's intention is to mock this ridiculous and obsessive behaviour as shallow.

Use in essays on…Illusion; Obsession; American Dream; Identity.

In an editorial on Lothrop Stoddard's *The Rising Tide of Colour*, The New York Times (1920) references,

"a new peril, that of an eventual submersion" of the "Nordics".

Interpretation: Meeting Nick for the first time in the novel, Tom references "The Rise of The Coloured Empires by this man Goddard" and claims, "if we don't look out the whole of the white race will be – utterly submerged." Fitzgerald clearly alludes to Stoddard's book, and uses Nick to subtly attack and belittle Tom's and Stoddard's views.

Analysis:

- The hyperbole of "utterly submerged" and the idea the book is "scientific stuff" highlight Tom's ignorance. Nick is "surprised" by Tom's tone; Daisy mocks Tom, saying, "we've got to beat them down" whilst "winking ferociously".
- Following WWI, race riots took place and Congress passed laws which set immigrant quotas. Here, Fitzgerald uses characters as vehicles to reveal and, in Nick, possibly undermine, white supremacist fears in America of "a new peril".
- Yet, Nick's description of Wolfsheim as a "flat-nosed Jew" reflects antisemitic views rife at the time. Indeed, Arthur Krystal argues Fitzgerald's descriptions of Wolfsheim, "if not triggered by anti-semitism, certainly emboldens it."

Use in essays on…Morality; American Dream; Power; Society.

James Truslow Adams (1931) coined the phrase 'The American Dream', claiming, "life should be better and richer and fuller for everyone, with opportunity for each according to ability or achievement."

Interpretation: Fitzgerald's novel alludes to, and criticizes, the concept of the American Dream and the false promise of the ideals it provided for Americans, particularly that of equality, regardless of social class or circumstances of birth.

Analysis:

- Using Gatsby's quest for Daisy, Fitzgerald criticises the credibility of the American Dream, portraying it as hollow and unachievable. It is rooted in the Declaration of Independence, which proclaims that "all men are created equal" with the right to "life, liberty and the pursuit of happiness."
- This dream relates to the idea of America as the Land of Opportunity, and states any man (note 'man'), if he is willing to work hard and improve himself, will find the means to do so there. One of the founding principles of the country is a firm belief in reward for hard work, and the idea of the Self-Made Man is one on which American values are fundamentally based.
- Those who have appeared to achieve the dream, 'winners' like Gatsby, would be seen as second-class citizens in East Egg. This is a reminder that the American Dream is fundamentally flawed and not available to everyone.

Use in essays on...Illusion; Obsession; Inequality; American Dream.

Paul L MacKendrick (1950) reminds us that,

"[F] Scott Fitzgerald at first intended to give the title *Trimalchio* to his novel *The Great Gatsby*."

Interpretation: Trimalchio references Petronius' *The Satyricon*. Trimalchio, an ex-slave who, through good fortune, managed to amass huge wealth, spends his time hosting lavish parties, trying to impress guests with manners and good breeding, yet falls far short of the standards of classical Rome.

Analysis:

- The allusion highlights the similarity between Trimalchio and Gatsby. *The Satyricon* was a satirical text; it mocked those who pretended to be more wealthy, educated, well-mannered, sophisticated and civilised than they actually were.
- Gatsby's nouveau riche wealth can never gain him acceptance into the world of the landed rich, represented by characters such as the Buchanans. Daisy comments that Gatsby resembles "the advertisement of the man", suggesting even she sees he is a facade. Readers may question such a barren and spiritually bereft life obsessed with appearances and based on materialism.
- What is the effect of changing the title from *Trimalchio* to *The Great Gatsby*, with its associations of showmanship and performance?

Use in essays on…Illusion; Identity; Materialism.

Robert Emmet Long (1966) makes the argument that,

"Part of the structural similarity then between *Heart of Darkness* and *The Great Gatsby* consists of the confrontation of two 'nightmares', one of the hero and the other of society, and of the choice finally made by the narrator in favour of the hero."

Interpretation: There are many similarities in the style and content of *The Great Gatsby* and Joseph Conrad's *The Heart of Darkness*; Conrad was a deep influence on Fitzgerald. Both narrators, when faced with a choice between a "nightmare" hero or society, choose the hero.

Analysis:

- Fitzgerald uses similar narrative methods to Conrad; *Heart of Darkness* is told, in part, by Marlow, a sympathetic narrator deeply involved in the plot, about the enigmatic and flawed Mr Kurtz. Like Gatsby, Kurtz has a dark side to his character and actions. Readers must be cautious to remember events are filtered through Nick (and Marlow), men who are deeply unreliable narrators.
- Nick's narration is often contradictory; what he tells the reader is a "choice". His character lacks self-awareness and awareness of the true nature of those around him.
- Despite choosing the "nightmare" hero, in both novels "society" brutally wins. Marlow learns "Mistah Kurtz – he dead", with the same finality Nick uses in his exclamation, "Mr. Gatsby's dead."

Use in essays on…Identity; Illusion; Power.

Judith Fetterley (1978) claims Daisy is the,

"object of the novel's hostility."

Interpretation: Fetterley condemns the male characters who objectify Daisy, who is then ultimately made a scapegoat for Gatsby's death. Nick's handshake with Tom ("I shook hands with him; it seemed silly not to") essentially absolves Tom of fault, leaving Daisy as the "object of the novel's hostility".

Analysis:

- Gatsby's ostentatious car is so recognisable, it arguably causes his own downfall and identifies him to Wilson. However, Fetterley proposes Daisy is to blame for Gatsby's death, since it is her who is driving, and she then partakes in the subsequent cover up which assures Wilson kills Gatsby.
- Daisy is never presented to feel guilty or take responsibility for her actions. This is compounded by the Buchanan's immediate departure ("she and Tom had gone away early that afternoon, and taken baggage with them") – if there was any guilt, the "baggage" was taken with her. Furthermore, Nick's condemnation is clear as Daisy "hadn't sent a message or a flower" to the funeral, instead retreating into the protection their wealth provides.

Use in essays on…Gender; Inequality; Wealth; Isolation.

James Hart (1986) characterised Gertrude Stein's 'Lost Generation' as those who, "rebelled against former ideals and values but could replace them only with despair or a cynical hedonism."

Interpretation: Stein famously asserted WWI had created a 'Lost Generation', a phrase Ernest Hemingway used in the epigraph to his novel, *The Sun Also Rises.* The phrase is particularly pertinent with regards *The Great Gatsby,* both in terms of characters' actions, and their motivations. It is important to question who is indeed "lost" in the novel.

Analysis:

- Fitzgerald critiques the post-war generation's lack of morality and purpose, reflected through numerous characters of all classes and genders, and "cynical hedonism" is evident throughout Gatsby's parties; yet, does Fitzgerald condemn some more than others?
- "Despair" is explicit in those such as Myrtle or Wilson, but to what extent does Fitzgerald highlight "despair" infiltrating the "ideals and values" of the upper class? Daisy and Jordan often express ennui, spending time lying around with nothing to do, yawning and asking, "What do people plan?" Since their lives are characterised by wealth and hedonism, they are entirely directionless and void of aspiration.

Use in essays on…Morality; Identity; American Dream; Society.

Lois Tyson (2006) called the novel a,

"scathing critique of American capitalist culture and the ideology that promotes it."

Interpretation: A Marxist reading of *The Great Gatsby* might focus on the gap between the rich and lower classes in post-war America; yet Fitzgerald highlights not only tension between classes, but also amongst the classes, as symbolised by East and West Egg.

Analysis:

- Fitzgerald gives a "scathing critique" of how the rich abuse others, seen in the desperate lives of the Wilson's scraping together a living in the dumping ground of 'The Valley of Ashes', and pitiful images of Wilson begging Tom for work.
- There was a certain alienation in society, a sense of purposelessness, as seen in Daisy; it resulted in a lack of personal fulfilment and focus on a hedonistic lifestyle. Money is a safety net to shield them from misdemeanours; even after framing Gatsby, they "retreated back into their money" without fear of reprisal.
- Fitzgerald criticises the careless, selfish and corrupt ruling class, revealing the American Dream to be a hollow illusion; characters are no more than "pulpless halves."

Use in essays on…Society; Materialism; Morality; American Dream.

Andrew Green (2018) argues that Gatsby himself is a, "composite of fragments."

Interpretation: Gatsby as a fragmented character is characteristic of the Modernist period and the "brokenness of the world" writers were trying to represent. TS Eliot describes this concept in *The Waste Land* as a "heap of broken images". The enigmatic mystery of Gatsby that perhaps makes him so "great" is that no one in the novel truly knows who the complete and authentic Gatsby is.

Analysis:

- Rumours of him as a "German spy", "Oxford man", and that he "killed a man" help this fragmentation. In Chapter 7, Daisy states "you're like the man in the advert"; even to her Gatsby appears as a simulation or façade.
- Nick even comments on Gatsby's affected "formality of speech"; that he "picks his words with care" hints his speech is part of a deliberately crafted persona.
- Gatsby's car is symbolic of his veneer, described as having, "a labyrinth of windshields that mirrored a dozen suns". The windshields and mirrors create an idea of reflections, like a hall of mirrors where one never gets a single authentic perspective; things are always skewed, and arguably this is what Gatsby does with his image.

Use in essays on... Illusion; Identity.

Davina Canham (2022) argues that,

"Fitzgerald uses Gatsby's character as a vehicle to expose the dark underbelly of American society."

Interpretation: As part of the bourgeoisie, Gatsby's wealth is amassed through business, not family inheritance. Whilst hinted at, the true nature of his business remains a mystery until we meet Mr Wolfsheim, and Tom reveals Gatsby's dealings with him as a way to discourage Daisy's interest, asserting "He and Wolfsheim…sold grain alcohol over the counter...I picked him for a bootlegger the first time I saw him".

Analysis:

- "Bootlegger", used disparagingly against Gatsby, reveals the corrupt side of Gatsby's carefully guarded veneer; his elegant parties, for instance, are built on phone calls where "Chicago was calling…on the wire" or "Philadelphia wants you on the phone", and we end with the report that "Young Parke's in trouble".
- Fitzgerald questions whether the American Dream could actually be achieved through honest hard work, or whether it was a facade for corrupt practices; the "the whisperings and the champagne and the stars" are built on people "looking for a business gonnegtion".

Use in essays on…Illusion; Identity.

Critical History

The Great Gatsby had many titles before Fitzgerald's publisher suggested the final choice; before that, *Trimalchio*, and even *Trimalchio in West Egg* had been working titles. "*In West Egg*" is interesting; whilst Fitzgerald is not Gatsby, parallels are evident, and *Trimalchio* places Fitzgerald's focus firmly on the individual; however, inclusion of "*In West Egg*" implies Fitzgerald is equally focused on the wider societal implications and discussions. A sense of not fitting in socially, or searching for one's place in the world – these themes are clearly of importance to Fitzgerald if they were to be in the title. "Great" in *The Great Gatsby* has far more positivity to it than *Trimalchio* does; associations of magic, showmanship and performance mean our protagonist is elevated to heroic status before we even begin.

Authors and critics lavished the novel with praise, yet Fitzgerald fixated on negative reviews. A thread through these criticisms was the implausible, unrealistic plot, something that frustrated Fitzgerald since, for him, the novel was always meant to be symbolic rather than literal. It is telling that Fitzgerald saw the novel as a romanticized version of reality; it implies admiration for Gatsby and his struggle in a world of make believe, much like Fitzgerald himself.

The novel's success grew when handed to soldiers during WWII to increase morale. Reception amongst troops brings to light many thematic concerns; were troops perhaps inspired by someone trying to win against all odds? Maybe determination and endeavour motivated readers; maybe the decadence and hedonism of Gatsby's world was a joyful relief.

The novel is open to exploration from numerous critical standpoints, but it is also useful to include literary contexts. The epigraph comes from *This Side of Paradise* and there are evident parallels in narrative structure to *Heart of Darkness*, areas ripe for discussion. Fitzgerald was also involved in Francis Cugat's iconic front cover, again allowing for interpretation of Fitzgerald's major motivations.

How to revise effectively.

One mistake people often make is to try to revise EVERYTHING!

This is clearly not possible.

Instead, once you understand the text in detail, a good idea is to pick five or six major themes, and four or five major characters, and revise these in great detail. The same is true when exploring key chapters – you are unlikely to be able to closely analyse every single line, so focus on the *skills* of analysis and interpretation and then be ready for any question, rather than covering the whole text and trying to pre-prepare everything.

If, for example, you revised Daisy and Power, you will also have covered a huge amount of material to use in questions about Wealth, Gatsby or Society.

It is also sensible to avoid revising quotations in isolation; instead, bring together two or three textual quotations as well as a critical and contextual quotation so that any argument you make is supported and explored in detail.

Finally, make sure material is pertinent to the questions you will be set. By revising the skills of interpretation and analysis you will be able to answer the actual question set in the exam, rather than the one you wanted to come up.

Suggested Revision Activities

A great cover and repeat exercise – Cover the whole page, apart from the quotation at the top. Can you now fill in the four sections without looking – Interpretations, Techniques, Analysis, Use in essays on…?

This also works really well as **a revision activity with a friend** – cover the whole page, apart from the quotation at the top. If you read out the quotation, can they tell you the four sections without looking – Interpretations, Techniques, Analysis, Use in essays on…?

For both activities, could you extend the analysis and interpretation further, or provide an alternative interpretation? Also, can you find another quotation that extends or counters the point you have just made?

Your very own Quotation Bank! Using the same headings and format as The Quotation Bank, find 10 more quotations from throughout the text (select them from many different sections of the text to help develop whole text knowledge) and create your own revision cards.

Essay writing – They aren't always fun, but writing essays is great revision. Devise a practice question and try taking three quotations and writing out a perfect paragraph, making sure you add connectives, technical vocabulary and sophisticated language.

Glossary

Alliteration – Repetition of the same consonant or sound at the beginning of a number of words in a sentence: the alliteration of the 'p' in "people played polo" creates a dismissive, belittling tone.

Allusion – Referring to something in a sentence without mentioning it explicitly: the description of "shouldered the mattress" could be an allusion to Christ carrying his crucifix, presenting Gatsby very much as an innocent victim.

Foreshadowing – When the writer alludes to or makes reference to something that is yet to come in the text: imagery of Gatsby stretching his arms towards the light emphasises his physical distance from Daisy, with "dark water" foreshadowing troubled times.

Hyperbole – An exaggerated statement that intensifies or adds emphasis: Fitzgerald further highlights the hedonistic and patriarchal nature of society through the idiom "world and its mistress", hyperbolically underlining the lack of morality and monogamy in society at the time.

Imagery – Figurative language that appeals to the senses of the audience: imagery of "foul dust" symbolises the American Dream itself.

Irony – A statement that suggests one thing but often has a contrary meaning: "imprisons" is ironic; it is the wealthy who are allegedly not free, suggesting wealth is a trap.

Juxtaposition – Two ideas, images or words placed next to each other to create a contrasting effect: the juxtaposition of "factual" and "imitation" is almost oxymoronic.

Language – The vocabulary chosen to create effect.

Metaphor – A word or phrase used to describe something else so that the first idea takes on the associations of the second: a "fairy's wing" is magical yet breakable. The metaphor highlights his dream is founded on something fragile or unrealistic.

Motif – A significant idea, element or symbol repeated throughout the text: Fitzgerald uses the motif of flowers (the "grotesque…rose" and "frightening leaves") and nature to present Gatsby's newly unsentimental view of the world.

Narrative Voice – The perspective (or 'voice') from which the story is told: Nick is the character invented to write the novel we read; it is important to remember everything that happens in the story is filtered through his character's perspective.

Repetition – When a word, phrase or idea is repeated to reinforce it: "Carelessness" is repeated, presented as a state of being for the rich where wealth allows them to commit immoral acts ("smashed up") without retribution.

Simile – A comparison of one thing with something of a different kind, used to make a description more vivid: Daisy is objectified, presented as attractive by Gatsby through the simile "gleaming like silver" as a trophy.

Symbolism – The use of a symbol to represent an idea: imagery of the "desolate path" is symbolic of the notion Gatsby has lost his way; the path to his dream is tarnished and hidden now.

Tone – The mood or atmosphere created by the writer: the list structure adds emphasis to Nick's tone of disgust, serving as an accumulation of negative points about the Buchanans.

Acknowledgements:

F Scott Fitzgerald: *This Side of Paradise,* published by Charles Scribner's Sons 1920
New York Times 1920
J Truslow Adams: *The Epic of America*, published by Little, Brown and Company 1931
P L MacKendrick: *The Great Gatsby and Trimalchio*, published by The Classical Association of the Middle West and South, Inc. 1950
R E Long: *The Great Gatsby and The Tradition of Joseph Conrad*, from *Texas Studies in Literature and Language Vol. 8, No. 3*, published by University of Texas Press 1966
J Fetterley: *The Resisting Reader: A Feminist Approach to American Fiction*, published by Indiana University Press 1978
J Hart: *The Concise Oxford Companion to American Literature*, published by Oxford University Press 1986
L Tyson: *Critical Theory Today*, published by Routledge 2006
A Krsytal: *Fitzgerald and the Jews*, published by The New Yorker 2015
A Green: *Fragmentation In The Great Gatsby: EMC emagazine 80,* published by the English and Media Centre 2018